At The Gate Called Beautiful

Precious Weddington

Copyright © 2016 Precious Weddington

All rights reserved. No parts of this book may be reproduced in any form by any electronic or mechanical means –except in case of brief quotations embodied in articles or reviews – without written permission from the publisher.

Copyright © 2016 Precious Weddington All rights reserved.
ISBN-10:0-692-66274-X
ISBN-13:978-0-692-66274-8

This book is a reminder to always walk in your calling, to stand in your purpose because no one else can do what you were created to do, and nobody can be who you were created to be. There is only one you, be the best you that you can be.

–For my children with love,

Mommy

Introduction:

Acts 3 New International Version (NIV)

Peter Heals a Lame Beggar
1 One day Peter and John were going up to the temple at the time of prayer—at three in the afternoon. 2 Now a man who was lame from birth was being carried to the temple gate called Beautiful, where he was put every day to beg from those going into the temple courts. 3 When he saw Peter and John about to enter, he asked them for money. 4 Peter looked straight at him, as did John. Then Peter said, "Look at us!" 5 So the man gave them his attention, expecting to get something from them.

6 Then Peter said, "Silver or gold I do not have, but what I do have I give you. In the name of Jesus Christ of Nazareth, walk." 7 Taking him by the right hand, he helped him up, and instantly the man's feet and ankles became strong. 8 He jumped to his feet and began to walk. Then he went with them into the temple courts, walking and jumping, and praising God. 9 When all the people saw him walking and praising God, 10 they recognized him as the same man who used to sit begging at the temple gate called Beautiful, and they were filled with wonder and amazement at what had happened to him.

Table of Contents

If I could Write 11

The Black Sheep 13

Close to Death 16

Misfit Mary 18

Why Would You Name Me… 19

A Heart of Worship 21

Brainstorming 22

A Letter to God 23

Tears Don't Lie 25

The Worse Part of Waking Up 27

The Angry Black Woman 29

The Great Illusion 32

Silenced Truth 35

The Crooked Side of Things 37

The Misinterpretation of a 'Ride or Die' 39

Forgotten Memory 40

Far.. 42

Fortified Sinner 44

Honest in the Pulpit 47

Reverberation 49

Crying Out with Purpose 50

If I could Write

If I could write
My fingers would paint words on blue skies of canvases
Draw up dreams with letters that come with distinct
animations that go beyond definition
No longer defined in syllables
The U's wouldn't be afraid to trust in the I am who gives us
meaning

If I could write
My paper would dance through rhythmic sequences of elegance to
capture the majestic
Crumble only as a sign of demonstration of knees bended
Lifted lines for the one on High in worship
My pen and paper would marry to share a covenant of promise to
speak truth
They'd be fruitful, multiplying continuously in understanding
Using voices to articulate how great He is

He

The I am
If I could write
I'd write love letters daily to love on him with language
Tactic fully use sentence structure to build up my vocabulary
for his majesty
Even though he already knows me
I'd use ink to dance on wings of notepads flying past my past and
into destiny

Greeting my now with who I am and who He created me to be
Written
Words spoken
I am His love splatter in perfection
Spoken without language

If I could write, I'd do it without pages
On opened land
With opened hand
And inked hearts

The Black Sheep

Broken like shattered glass on streets that bleed graffiti
She walks restless relentlessly searching for answers that school can't give her

She's confused

In a world that calls 'pink' 'blue' but can't distinguish fact from truth
Her eyes narrow like the blunt she just hit with a two by four forcing memories of present pains through lungs she refuses to take breaths to scream with

Her insides burning for freedom but chaos ransacks her 10' by 11' bedroom that hums from the smell of adolescence, clothes thrown into piles of hatred for herself
Black was never her favorite color
Until her wool was dyed by foes of friends who said they were friends and to keep her enemies' closer
Backwards
This system of beliefs held by the majority of people endlessly searching for the same thing: hope

Music pumping through beats that beat her insanely into thinking popularity is a contest worth winning
Even when the biggest loser can become famous, jokes don't seem as comedic but become cynical
Her life
Nothing more than inanimate seconds dwindling

down every moment into milliseconds of dust

Ashes to ashes
Dust to dust

Death happens to all men

But how do you live?
Because the practice suicide notes in her desk drawer lets her know she is not excluded from the cycle
And to her dying seems so easy in a place where the living walk around in grave clothes
Weighed down by failures and regrets
Drowning in hatred, being smothered by greed and gluttony
What's the point of living without true happiness?

Money can't seem to buy love
In a place where money rules everything after it answers all needs
While pews are indoctrinating by messages of prosperity
Has her questioning…who she is really serving
Who is really her master?
She once considered herself a masterpiece
Until other pieces made by the Master ripped sections from her life that once highlighted the beauty in her eyes
Now shaded by sleepless nights and tears drowning the joy of living

What's the point in living anymore?

Her failures drew pictures of her future, and she believed them

Believed that her worth was measured by success
and dollars signs that read in green
Instead of seeing in red

Red streams of blood that pour daily by a continually crucifixion without surrender
Christ, constantly loving through open wounds of beaten hearts that resist him
Afraid to face Him
Or even acknowledge His existence

He's persistently pursuing her passionately

And she hasn't even recognized it

Her life more valuable than she can imagine
He's paid the price for it
His sacrifice made mention in living documents
No fairy tale
No beautiful images…just a life for a life
Death for the living
Somebody should probably tell her that when he said it was over…
It was finished
So her aimless searching is over
He found her that day on the cross
He was nailed into 2 by 4's for the high she wants to use to ease the pain
He can ease the pain
She's not the black sheep in his family
She's the one he's left the other 99 to find
He won't ever leave her
Somebody should tell her

Close to Death

I glanced at his arms
Scars like map quest
Mapping to his soul
Needles...became arrows
Leading demons to the destination that he calls Home

There, he invited them
Only because to him...they seem like company
You know what they say about misery
He miserably exposed himself to me
Lifted shirts and shared stories
Opened wounds...like slitting his wrist before me
He promised not to trip...too far down memory lane
While I held his hand
Letting his tears nourish the ground that been starving of nourishment
His feelings dry and cracked like his skin
I felt it
Through finger tips that touched dry lips with a verbal kiss
Of life...
He'd died so many times
That life, seemed like a distant memory
Clouded vision from down spiraling hopes and smoked up dreams
He allowed me to speak life
And I cradled the life in me
Sought His help so I could see
What it was that He'd have me speak
And begin speaking
Using the authority to plant seeds of living

Watching the seeds take root with each tear

Watering the future and washing away the past

His last
Experience of hope was destroyed by false prophesy
But I wasn't speaking prophetically
Rather truth that can't be destroyed
His life was a tool
That God was ready to use
Forget the confusion …Satan had so long tried to confuse
Telling him that he was worthless
That he had no purpose
That everything that he did was a silly mistake
Because his parents didn't love him
So every attempt to make them happy
Seemed to be drowned by the issues that they had to face
So they seemed to forget his face
And when he got old enough to fill the emptiness
He felt empty

Misfit Mary

I just want to hear your voice
Silence the thoughts that scream for my attention
Thoughts that tell me to seek different

I just want to lay at your feet and listen

Use my hair to soak in your presence because I just want to be near you
Let every follicle embrace your grace like conditioner
conditioning my ears to hear your voice
Your sheep know your voice
So I need to practice listening to be sure I'm hearing you when you're speaking
I'll break open my box full of fragrance in hopes it'll be a sweet, sweet savor to your nostrils
Cry out in silence
Let the laborers work
I just want to be near you
To hear you
Breathing life back into to me
My life has been so empty
Lord empty me
So I can feel you
Fill me
I may look out of place
But I'm in the right place
At your feet
At your throne
Bended
Box broken open

Why Would You Name Me…

I can imagine the doctor's response to pronouncing it
Hands covering mouths with small attempts to not laugh
Probably thinking "and why would you name her this"
 In a society of predisposed opinions always offered on street corner offices
Labels
Sticky noted to forever "Racial Profiling"
Because there is no way I can hide behind a name
A bold statement of meaning but clearly assigned to a certain criteria of people
I'm prejudged based on letters in the alphabet forming an adjective
If you ask me
I'm not content with it
Precious
Movie madness on the T.V
Striking hood gimmicks and memes
Questions like "your mother must of really loved you, huh?"

"No my dad actually named me"

Every name says something about you
Your name carries weight
So when people hear my name they immediately think of cute and cuddly things
"Aww…I named my puppy that"
As if I'm supposed to smile

Or think it's cute
But really it's my name, not a nickname that everyone just decided to give to me

And certainly not one to be compared to your puppy
I use to feel really angry with a name like mines
Thinking that it was a sure guarantee to have me compartmentalized
A sure agent of criticism to keep me from venturing into places that would otherwise be deemed as not for me
And certainly…a name should not carry such ability
But a name
There is something about a name
A word that you respond to
A description without definition that you give definition to
Your name may be someone else's but you wear yours differently
You wear yours intimately
Your name
Places you in a place that belongs to you
A space in time allotted to you
Your Name
Bears witness of your character traits
Your name
Given for a specific reason
Shameless
So wear it with confidence
You are what you answer to
And your name is yours
Embrace it

A Heart of Worship

There is a tempo my pen dances to
On plains that glisten with hope
Decorated by words that give life to empty vessels rattled by dead bones in valley where there once was war
My ink shed like blood rushing through veins of blue that run through blank canvases of open notebooks
And in those pages reside my heart of worship

If my lead could lift hands in ripples of vowels vowing to honor the life breathed into them through grace
If they could use hyperboles to get down on bended knees…
Every ounce of my journals' being would gravel in admiration
Like the pages to my diary
Writing history of how wonderful His love is for me
My highlighters would sing hymns of ambiance to adorn
His Majesty
My doodles would bring gifts of creativity for His creative greatness when forming me
These words would collaboratively take turns expressing syllables of symbols upon cymbals that play effortlessly in reverence to Him

Musically without music singing, "Master of the universe, Lord of all the Earth! I give all my praise to you because only you are worthy"
My pencil honors Him in tones of gray, writing in tunes to perfume any room He's willing to come into

I want to be a sweet aroma to Him
Let my notebook speak of my heart
Draw it upon lines like sheets of music…singing silently
My heart of Worship

Brainstorming

The thought hit me hard
And I'm almost certain I was caught in a storm of emotions
Clouding my perception
Like a tornado devastating land, I hadn't even tilled

Somethings are just easier to forget

Unless they leave an imprint like lightning bolts and barbed wire on dark nights
Of walking through farm lands getting struck by shattered horizons
I'm just a person with a pen
Painting words on canvases of ears
Hoping it penetrates the mind like a dagger
Have you ever been struck by someone else's electricity?
Body absorbing the intensity of their frequency
Almost like a sponge in the middle of a storm while it's pouring
Like my tears...warring
With my face
The silent beat of eternity tapping underneath my eye lids
Puddles of life created from storms of misunderstood
clouds that shade underneath my pride
Drowning the sound of the call
"Many are called" but don't know how to answer
Sending text messages asking questions to Jeeves
Who uses my confusion to tweet
While Google Earth searches for solutions for me
No one can save me
I'm stuck in this storm
Brainstorming

A Letter to God

I wrote God a letter the other day
Sat down with seriousness in my ink and said
"Look now, Lord you have to hear what I'm about to say, in this letter."
"Life just ain't getting any better for me"
It read
My ink bleeding onto my soul with the heart of my lead

"God, do you understand?
The world doesn't love me, but the men do
Although they show it in five minute visits, hour long sittings, and tattered linens…
They aren't exactly faithful
My girls
They paint me these vivid pictures of movies and a dinner
Overeat the media just to get thinner
Then tell me it's more exciting than it looks
So I put on my "ready for action" outfit
Take a step out there and every critic can swear that the world just doesn't care about me
But the truth is…well yeah, I guess that is the truth
Yet for some odd reason I can't see you
I can't hear you, smell you
But Lord I can feel you
I can feel you more than that guy that just filled me up to capacity
I can feel every ounce of your love for me
Like rivers of living water flowing
I can feel you more than my girl on MTV talking about the reason she don't have a man is because all they do is cheat

I feel you
But I don't think…. you 'feelin' me"

I paused to let my ink think

Because the tears began to flow and the words bled from the scarred hole in my soul
"God you know me
Better than I know myself
But it seems from every breath, all I'm doing is destroying me
I no longer look at sin as a disease
Rather an incorporative friend that satisfies my fleshy need
God please, let your judgment see fit to elect me
Like a wayward child whose run away from home, correct me
Just please, please don't forget me
You said you'd never leave me, nor forsake me
So God please…understand me
I'm writing through hyperboles that dialogue my reality
While symbolically exposing my morality
Because I have sinned
And I need you to forgive me"

I wrote a letter to God the other day
Sat down with seriousness in my ink and said
"Look now, Lord you have to hear what I'm about to say, in this letter."

Tears Don't Lie

I have cried before
Tears drenching the pillow like floods caused by hurricanes that
drown sea shores
I am not numb
My heart beats just as loudly as the person standing next to me

So don't think that I feel nothing

I feel everything

Like the whispers that shove its voice down the throat of
knifes that stab me in the back
I hear keenly

Believe me

I might not know every word that's spoken
But I know there are plenty against me
I am an advocate of hope
I believe in peace
I know that struggle exist

So I pray without cease
And my prayers are heard
I'm sure of it

So despite those who question if my God exist
He continues to prove it
I am only on the witness stand to speak of it
And I know the world can be a cold place
I live in it

Breathe the same air you breathe
See the things you see

My heart is broken daily by the pressure of society

And because there is no peace this world offers,
I find it in Jesus

The Worse Part of Waking Up

Maybe she woke up with eyebrows perfectly aligned with
cheekbones that favor blush on its own
Hair lay gently in curls of wavy convenience
Skin clear and bright like an early spring morning

Fresh

Not a scar or blemish that's noticeable to the naked eye so
her waking up seems beautiful
Flawless almost except her last night was far from it
Waking up to broken promises in bed next to dead dreams
All she remembers was the drinks
And he's sound asleep
Eyes shut too tightly to see her radiance so it goes unnoticed
Except for the reflection from a mirror that reminds her she's
accepted by many but appreciated by little

Her perfect complexion and tiny yet curvy frame, delicately fitting
into silk gown that compliments her personality
She's the video vixen without the T.V. screens
The "beautiful enough for the movies"
The exotic beauty
But her bed sheets tell stories of fallen soldiers that claimed the
desire to conquer but were only stationed

Woke up with no makeup but face painted with yesterday's sorrows
Those that were drowned out by last night shenanigans
Her independence a cover up because cover girls makes the
most sense
But what makes change?
Because her reflection screamed social beauty but her life
wore pain on the inner seams of her dreams

She wanted to be a wife
To be a mother

But after one too many written good night stories her book seemed too full for her bed
And her need to be "The One" …they all wanted, made her seem less appealing to that one

The One

Her sweet dream became a beautiful nightmare
Trading her perfect ability to be herself perfectly
To be what she thinks everyone else wants her to be
Played as the background music to her background music

She

Can't see her own beauty in reflections
Daily looking in mirrors but seeing worthless
But her worth is in the one who created her
Heart ready to save her
He is not just the Captain
He created the seas

And the fish that is meant for her will be patiently waiting

Because He makes all things new
Renewed
If only she would look into His mirror
Behold Him beholding her
Beauty is in the Eyes of the Beholder
And she is the apple of His Eye
She can sleep more peaceful
Because the mornings won't be so hard anymore

The Angry Black Woman

They call her angry
Mouth full of brimstone fire
Hellish with words that could burn holes in any man's soul

She's ferocious

Like a lioness in mid hunt, seeking to dismember her prey
And I can't help but wonder if they tell her story with details to help outline why her words seem so dishearten
Sublime to wisdom and easily filled with pain
They say that black women are the hardest to get along with
Say there are walls built up around their hearts that are built with vocabulary
Tell me that their attitudes make them too strong willed
Undesirable to most men
Who view them as un-submissive
And I look back through history
Dead beat daddies that raped their great- great- great grandmothers out of acts of pure lust on a regular basis
Then watched them be whipped, spit on and downgraded by white women because their skin became objects of affection to "their" men
Dragged and hung from telephone poles and bridges for carrying "their" children without being asked to share their bodies

I don't believe we're angry
Just hurt
Taught without words directly to be strong because once upon a time our beauty made us the enemy in a country that thought less of us

Call it three strikes if you'd like

Which makes it more evident
Prisoners in a place they never asked to be
Drug, raped, beat helplessly, humiliated in streets to prove they were only pieces of meat
And they wonder why so many are seen as angry

Why some misuse their bodies
Because that's what they inherited
Lost files of American history
Telling stories of men who told their daughters they were only useful to them for one thing after trading their mothers off to please wives who had grown to hate them even more
Spoke daily over young black females calling them whores
Yet they wonder why tough skin was the outcome
After being whipped with cattails was outlawed, harsh treatment with words became prevalent
And they made sure to make them out to be irrelevant
Ignored their beauty and made a mockery of it
Maybelline sure knew how to make our lips seem too big
Most lay down on tanning beds to try to get this brown skin
Advertisements rarely showing our faces but
somehow plastic surgery made our features blossom on faces that had never known the true beauty of them
Slowly integrated us through "color"
Lighter shades first
Billboards that accentuate their bodies while making sure to show most of our negative outbreaks
Making sure to show us shaking it for some dollars just to keep us chained
Making slaves once again
But our slick mouths and tough skin fight to not let them
So now our freedom isn't forfeited, it's just delayed
Now it's not them that's holding us captive, it's our inability to forgive that has us in chains
We're bound by the pain

Silent upbringing teaching us to be independent with castrated hands
No longer anger, but fear that keeps us locked away
In our own personal space
We hide ourselves from healing
The world is hateful
But love is perfect
We are loved perfectly
So let's forgive
And stop being "angry"

The Great Illusion

Step right up!
Come, view the most amazing
Incredible
Astonishing act ever seen by men
One so bold
So moving
So exhilarating it could almost cause one to
...to believe

A mere man

Stretched across wood, nailed, bloody, swollen, beaten and bruised
Dying
And this book says he did it for you

What fool wrote this?

The son of God
God
What God?

You are in control of your own lives
And sin
Sin is a lie crafted by men who designed morals as a conditioning tool to control the masses
A long wooden spoon fed to you by men who believe that there is a distinct difference between good and evil
That there is a soul inside of you
That destiny has to exist otherwise nothing would be in existence

"Come right on up...
See him "

This flesh man

Hanging
Disfigured

Now
Let me place this curtain before you
Between you and him

Viola!

Can you see him anymore?

Smoke screens and antics fight for our attention among audiences of hypnotized people
Mind control at its best
Only the control is handed over willingly
"Show me proof that God exist and I'll believe, because truth is relative."
So we look for what we can relate to
Like magicians we walk around with our wands
Powerless
Eyes glued to kaleidoscope dreams that keep switching
So while we're watching one thing, the real thing is overshadowed by distraction
The same strategy that an enemy use
If I can convince you to focus on something different
It's as if the real thing isn't there

Watch me

Present you with so much truth you'll have knowledge of most things

But still you'll question
God's authority
His necessity

You'll have access to the greatest proof
But you'll use it as data for researching
I'll give you mock resources, for temporary things
Information to create even more blinders that you'll willingly place on yourself and others
Because now you believe
And much like a magician
I've deceived you

Silenced Truth

Sometimes I watch
Almost in tears because there's so much I wish I could tell them
So much I wish I could show them in four minutes of
uninterrupted visits of their words interjecting into mine
But I'm sure they won't listen
Minds made up of decisions
Preconceived before any words were mentioned so the tension grows
Before I'm even able to say "You mean something" Somehow my
expectations only remind them of where God wants to guide them
and they hate being reminded of the truth
So I feel like one forced to watch them play the fool
The tool used to slow down progress in their lives
Sometimes I want to scream
Lift my voice in a fit of rage because I know some know what's
really happening but keep provoking the wrath of
God on their lives because they lack understanding

I can't even imagine what God's feeling
When we deliberately do the opposite of what He asks us to
Forfeit our gifts for worldly profit
This means nothing when we lose our souls
Stand proud of our lives while making proclamation of control

How bold we must believe we are

To sin so earnestly
Without fear of the Almighty
The Everlasting
We…
Act as if eternity is momentary

As if forever is merely a word used to simply enlarge our view of life when dying

There is no end to it

Yet we live as if we're living in it
Sometimes my heart is broken for those who think God is just something to be played with
Some cosmic demonstration, left for personal interpretation
After a lack of consideration, we try to make Him into whatever suits our desperation
Without desperately seeking Him
And for those speaking truth…we desperately silence them
For fear of "real recognizing real"

Yet His grace is sufficient

Willing to cover us even when we haven't asked to acquire the coverage
He's guaranteed insurance
Assuring that no matter the cost, he's already made the payment
And regardless of delinquent accounts, He's in the business of savings
I'm always amazed at those who can hear of His goodness
and still choose to renounce it

Walk away, to walk back to it
To walk away again
Those who profess Him but won't accept
The truth

The Crooked Side of Things

I can see her smiling next to highlights that outline his boredom
This looks like a game
And I'm one of the referees kicked out for actually calling foul plays and trying to go by the book

This process took me much longer than I am proud to admit and so in defense:
This just isn't it
I keep trying to keep my two cents pocketed for fear of rejection and hopes of some sort of epiphany that can't be bought with a veil, bouquet, and a dream

"WAKE UP, THIS AIN'T REAL!"

I sometimes feel like the crazy one for keeping silent in movie theaters when the girl runs into the arms of the killer

"No girl, run!!
That's him.
He's in yo kitchen girl! Eating yo food! Girl, now he's in yo bathroom using yo shower, his clothes are lining your laundry basket.
Girl run! Run! Run!
He gon' kill you!"

And as much as I want to scream at screens that are only for viewing

I don't
I just eat my hot tamales and keep watching because nobody asked me for my two cents

Even when I paid to watch it
Even when I'm obviously given the ability to see what is bound to happen right in front of me
My lips keep shut
Like a vow of silence almost
To avoid rejection
It's almost like knowing an alternate route
But having to mime the directions
To someone who blindfolded themselves and then put me on mute

The Misinterpretation of a 'Ride or Die'

She's willing to die for him

And not one of those honorable deaths that could award her a Purple Heart

But one that would cause her to lose everything in life but her life

And for some reason, she thinks it's honorable

So she's suited up in camouflage and boots for a man who can't give direct orders

She's wandering aimlessly, confused

Fighting battles on fields full of land mines that he's set

…with his misuse of true leadership

Yet she follows his orders like a Lieutenant

Faithful to her "Sargent"

While he's unsure of his Commander

She waits for his command

Fighting battles for territory that doesn't belong to them, to him, to her

She thinks she's winning the small ones, but she's already lost the war

Forgotten Memory

Silent
Like dark corners in rooms that bear resemblance to faces bruised by finger prints
Bodies laid across pieces of fabric wrapped in warped dreams...dreaming through closed eyes counting sheep they just slept with

I'm alone

In a room full of people dreaming of better while trying to figure out how to live better
Is better really better or is it just a painted version of lies with pretty colors to disguise the darkened rooms with corners where bodies lie

Dead

But breathing

I'm concerned that our idea of life has become just a modification of death
Like the autumn colors that seem vibrant but really represent decay
We keep going this way
This way
These alleys keep echoing a truth

To "stay out of the darkness, there are monsters there"
Hungry for feeding just to be eating dreams we keep dreaming while lying in their corners

DYING

Tell me
Why must my eyes be closed while in the corners being raped by a system that throws bright paint on the walls surrounding me
As if I can see the death I'm lying on top of
As if decay smells any different than the garbage I'm being fed
All I know it is trash
In darkened corners
On piles of bodies I keep counting
My body count is massive
Mostly because I couldn't see the harm it was doing to them or me
Killing for dreams that are dying in me

Far

Far
Like distant memories clearing cloudy skies in mid-June
How are thunderstorms forming on the horizon of clear skies in July?

My summer sped through like Friday afternoons
While I'm wondering the cost of dripping pipes that run water
for cities that clean relentlessly for dirty
people...washing to get clean
My tub stained by my insane attempts to clear my skin of fake beauty
Rubbed on by faulty women that script to me how to be a wife
To a husband that society says needs a freak and 'classy' all tied in one
Along with motherly instincts

Oh...did I mention how racked my brain is?

From counting diapers that blue lines streak as often as the flash of my camera
Trying to make sure I don't miss a thing
Yet I keep forgetting to cook dinner

I forgot to cook dinner

Covered in saliva and wishful thinking of days for just me
Daydreaming of oatmeal mixtures that somehow end up on my face, but not like a spa treatment

I can't even have my daydreams to myself because I wake up next to him...or him
I'm not complaining, merely explaining the truths

Mommy, wifey, ma ma, wife, she, me, we...no 'I' in team

So there is no time for me

Sleep seems like holidays
It only comes for special occasions
Over emphasize its nature, and then leave me almost instantly in bed next to dad and baby sound asleep
While my mind has recorded a million and one things throughout the day that it's playing

Like thoughts on high speed chases

Arrested with no rest

Fortified Sinner

It's like it's engraved in stone
Or declared among Congress
Like an investigation proudly closed because of a sufficient amount of evidence
A fortified sinner with very little leverage
And I don't say that proudly
Rather speaking openly screaming

WARNING

Because grace and mercy is what's keeping me
But for some odd reason all I can see is a good feeling
    It feels good
      He smells good
      Taste so good
      Walk so good
      Talk so good
"It's all good" …except it's not
Because for each 'feel good'
It's like tipping Satan for a glass of misery with a death shot
Or should I say a death wish
Which he'd be more than willing to grant if given the opportunity
But it's not my time yet
So he keeps bugging God with schemes and plots on how to get to me
And it's stupid because even with all the knowledge that I have….
I just keep falling

And you would think that with all the years of experience
I'd be a fortified solider
Instead of a fortified sinner
Fighting for the Kingdom of God instead of helping my enemy become a winner

Using the tools given to me to walk away from sin
To resist temptation
But instead you'll catch me
Criticizing the music I listen to just to two step to its melody
I know it sounds as if I'm speaking hypocritically
Truthfully, I am not
But that's what my life seems to show
A Christian with morals and values
But if you're cute and do right I might just take off some clothes
Don't get passive aggressive, this is what sinners do
Don't look at me funny, I'm only speaking the truth
And the truth is that our excuse is

"I'm not perfect, no one is"

But that mentality is probably the one thing that causes us to sin
1 John 1 and 8-9 states
 If we say we have no sin, we deceive ourselves and the truth is not in us
But if we confess our sins he is faithful and just to forgive us

Let me not speak for everyone else
Let me allow this piece to speak by exposing myself
Jill Scott said "You ain't no saint, we all are sinners"

So I guess that meant it was ok to sin
So I took an ounce of the sex drug

Smoked a little
Puff puff passed it
And that's when death began
But a life for a life is how the story ends
And striving daily to live righteous is covered through blood that covers my torn painting
He remakes me daily

So even though I fail him often
I confess often
Not to be sinless…but to sin less

Honest in the Pulpit

Can I use contractions as a metaphor to describe this throbbing
pain in the pit of my stomach when I get like this?
This moment where salvation is standing next to me but I can't feel
it where I'm standing
In a state of falling with ground directly underneath me

[I wish I could completely describe]

This state of mind I'm in
Where the word becomes the vomit on my pillow case at night
where I lay
Leaving my face stained with glory, but a soul empty
Ask me, have I ever faked hand lifting
And I'll explain that at times I don't feel God and although
I know He's not a man, so he can't lie
Sometimes I question if He's with me
Or if when He says he loves me despite of my flaws if He really
means it
Because right now I feel so filthy

Covered in grime
I'd be surprised if he can even see me beneath all my lies
Buried under false identities, drenched in smiles that don't mean
anything other than fake happiness and alternative meanings

I still deal with idol wondering

My mind often takes off like a rocket ship
Leaving me spaced out without being high
Enough to dilute my memory
Remembering all that I did the night before
Temper tantrum
And it's not one of those extremely noticeable ones

It's one of those ...If I had a toy
I'd probably throw it across the room
And it would be safe to assume
That I could care less if it hurt anyone in its path
Finding a landing spot
In the mist of unnecessary issues
You could hear me screaming

Silently

Among the walls of extremity
Because a part of me is angrily
Expressing itself through blank stares and painting
Check the facial expression: blankly
Like a blank piece of paper
Used for anything
Not necessarily meant for meaning
My blank stares are merely
Pieces of anger
Writing stages of what pain is
Painting
If there were extra
Then the paint brush of my tantrum
Would be
Dull
Null and void
Sort of like my feelings are to other's currently
I'm on the waves of this current and we

Are about ready to wash other's up onto shore
Expose them for what they really are

But love covers a multitude of sin

Reverberation

I took my ear from the streets
Took the cord from my vocal cords so they wouldn't hear me
Or feel me...vibe with me
I sound proofed my lyrics
So the base in my base lines wouldn't be too loud for you to hear
Him when He speaks
I've come to realize it's not about me
So I can either conform to the worldly way of thinking
Or I can be like Optimus Prime transforming
Let his love transform me

Behold all things are new

Old things have passed away
Like conversations mentioning dead things
Pass acknowledging that the existence of a thing is no longer
So I can no longer hold on to things that are meant to be dead
I will no longer bury my God and his ordinances under this flesh
I am in this world but not of it so I'll disconnect
My controller no longer connected to this X Box
X marks the spot for demise
And the box meaning to lay this flesh to rest
So I've given up the former way of life
No longer controlled by this corrupt world
Dominated by Satan's lies
Life ain't a game
But I'll let He that lives within me control it just the same

Crying Out with Purpose

The issues of life just dried up on the patch of skin underneath my eye lash
And the forecast of my current situation is a reflection of my past

Looking right at me

They say that tears can heal a broken heart
But my heart is still broken
And I'm
I'm still crying
My eyes almost bleeding

It started simply
Simply crying
Eyes full of tears used to drown out fears
I felt my stomach turn flips
Churning with the pain that had no name
Lost in understanding
Standing in a river forgetting how to swim
Because all I could feel
Were the tears

Have you ever cried so hard your head hurts?

Throbbing from the misery of misunderstanding
Tired of trying to think
Tired of trying to feel past the feeling
Tired of trying to see past the present

Eyes swollen from desperately seeking vision through clouded understanding

"If only I could touch him"

Voice crackling under the pressure
The pressure to be silent when you really want to scream
The hope of guidance

When it seems…all hope is lost
Looking through a window pane
Remembering the dreams that once set the standards in reality
Allowing what seems to comfort you momentarily
To wash over the pane
Gently removing the stains
Only leaving trails of broken promises

I've cried a river
Flooded my life with worries (worthless)
Watched my pain exchange its name
For no value or purpose
But Lord my tears
They seem to drown me
Lost in the motions, feeling low and hopeless
Needing a touch from you

All I need is for you to touch me
Turn my sorrow and weeping
Into joy
Bottled up…
Suppressed feelings
Into open ministry
Use the tears to free me
Open my eyes to see clearly

"I can see clearly now the rain is gone"

But rain on me

Use my tears to wash the filth used to keep me

Dirty images of what use to bind me
Old lies used against me
Tattered goals used to remind me

Of what I thought I should be
Let the tears flow like the rainy season
Let them season me
Rinsing over my soul to create a clean heart in me
Renew my mind with the peace you've given me
The tears like a silent stream restoring me

There is purpose in crying

Even when you can't see past the frame
The rain may seem to make the window blurry
Hard to characterize objects in motion
But the tears serve a purpose
To wash away the grime
To cleanse your memory
To help you see clearly the necessary defenses
Defending your mind from invasion
Irrigating lands that you thought were deserted
Meeting your desperation
Lord do open heart surgery on your patient
I'm waiting
Eyes…vision…directed toward destiny
The tears flowing easily
Like the rivers of the living

Living

Living tears…no longer water wasted
But a source used to heal

Vision

Lord I'm crying
Crying…crying out with purpose

Tears of sorrow
Turned into tears of life
Weeping may endure for a night

But joy comes in the morning light
Blinded but now I see
The dryness of darkness lifted
Pain to gain …shifted
Cause I'm crying out with purpose

www.ingramcontent.com/pod-product-compliance
Lightning Source LLC
Chambersburg PA
CBHW031433040426
42444CB00006B/790